# A Safe Place

**Rhapsody**
61 Gainsborough Road, Felixstowe, Suffolk
IP11 7HS

ISBN 1 898030 34 0

British Library Cataloguing in Publication Data
available.

Cover illustration by Tony Botterill

Printed in Kent by JRDigital Print Services

Author Publishing Ltd reprinted January 2004

These poems are for all the special
people in my life.

Some here, some already in heaven.

They know who they are.

'A Safe Place' is Jo Harrison's first book. She was born in Shipston-on-Stour, Warwickshire. She grew up happily in Newport,Pembrokeshire with her parents, sister and brother, and an assortment of much-loved dogs and cats. She now lives in Felixstowe with her lovely husband and two gorgeous children.

In 1998 she was disagnosed with breast cancer. The sometimes painful, often joyful, and always precious years since have been a revelation of love and affection. Care and kindness arrived constantly, in many forms, from devoted family, friends, church family and even friends of friends. Sharing these poems is a way of 'giving something back'.

Her words are inspired by a huge love of God and fuelled by a desire to make a difference for the good.

1 Peter 4 v 10 - N.I.V. Bible

'Each one should use whatever gift he has received to serve others, faithfully administering God's grace in its various forms.'

# Poems

# Trusting God in the Tough Times

## Isiah 46 v 4

## 'I have made you and I will carry you'

1

## Grace in Weakness

Treading water in the deep end
We're unwilling to take a dive.
The trials of this life cannot submerge
Our passionate will to survive.

Claiming the promise of Jesus,
"My grace is sufficient for you,
My power is made perfect in weakness."
We trust him to carry us through.

Our smiles must not be waterlogged,
God's warmth we can always impart.
We'll patiently wait for the tide to turn,
Composed and with love in our hearts.

Our sweet reward will be heaven
A golden celestial crown,
But for now we shall tread water calmly,
Our lifeguard will not let us drown.

### Resolve

Full up with love
Full up with words
Full up with tears
Unshed.
Primed explosively
To dissolve my resolve
To be strong
And to stay
And to do it God's way.
Give me the strength Lord, please,
Give me the strength for today.

## Sublime Wishes

Sublime wishes are hard to offer
But offer them we must,
When peace for those we love
Is so much more important
Than dreams we dare to dream,
Which may never take priority
This side of eternity.

So where to go from here?
Just to go on doing good
And being kind
And filling people's hearts
With warmth and peace
And smiles,
And sunshine for the darkest days.

Shine like stars
Think noble thoughts,
Salt to the earth
And light to the night
And keep on trying.
It will all be all right in the end,
It has to be.

## Flying the Flag

She remains on earth,
Breathing in seasons
Of hazy hallowed time.

Her tenacious will
Fighting to endure
The effort to survive.

To be purposeful
In 'flying the flag'
For the innocent lost.

All of her being
She offers for them,
Trusting that they are safe.

All of her being
She offers for them,
Using her life to love.

## The Proverbial Wall

Suddenly nobody loves you
You've told them they mustn't call
Feelings trip over emotions
As you hit the proverbial wall.

No-one is indispensable
Other lives go on fine after all
Leaving behind a muddled soul
Who has hit the proverbial wall.

Viewing the depth of the black hole
You want to curl up in a ball
The outside world is so scary
When you hit the proverbial wall.

You shy away from all contact
It's best they don't see you fall
Tears can be shed in private
As you face the proverbial wall.

Your strength will be gathered softly
With this rest away from the toil
And slowly time will help you scale
That wretched proverbial wall.

## Bright Darkness

It's hard to shine
When you are all alone
In a room full of people.

It's hard to be a bright light
In the darkness
However bright that darkness is.

It's hard to understand
Why I miss you this much
But I do.

So I trust God to know
And I just go on loving
Whilst He lights my way
One day
At a time.

**The Only Way**

Dogged kindness is the only way
Boundless love in the face of pain
Reaching out with tenderness
Again and again and again

Compassion to cushion crisis
Gentle smiles to ease the strain
Using our gift of time to care
Again and again and again.

'Trust in the Lord with all your heart,'
His message is still the same,
Love and love and love and love
Again and again and again.

## Let Them Laugh

The crushing sadness of remembrance
Hit us full on again today.

The assault held at bay
Only by passionate purpose.

We *must* make it right for the children.

Watch them choose bright blooms with care
And pen sweet messages
In their very best, childish hand.

Paint a sunny picture of Mum
Smiling at her colourful crew
Dodging showers and placing flowers
In a sodden Springtime cemetery.

Hold on tight to their hands and hearts
And let them laugh.

We *must* make it right for the children.

## Someone is Missing

Another crazy year slips by
And more explosions pass
We go on playing leading roles
In life's peculiar farce.

The missing hurts us all at times
And questions still abound
Our prayers revealing answers
We still strive to understand.

Do you get to see us all?
Is peace your hard fought share?
And do we love them well enough
The ones left in our care?

Once more we saw the fireworks
Bright hope to light the skies
Hot dog treats and happiness
And radiant, wondrous smiles.

Candy floss and kindness
Rich affection all around
A small boy's indoor refuge too
From night and cold and sound.

Plastic rainbow halos shine
On fur lined princess hats
New memories in the making now
What would you think of that?

United by your absence
Loving babes you held so dear
Our families walk together
Towards another precious year.

## Hopeful Hearts

The sadness is appalling
Despite the love around.
No words are quite sufficient
To explain the sombre sound
Of lonely, helpless hours
Spent emotionally drowned.

Sometimes it's impossible
To go on being strong,
We know the prize is heaven
But the road is very long.
The challenge is accepting
That our weakness is not wrong.

We struggle to continue
Though the fight is really hard
We want to be triumphant
And we will, with faith our guard,
But first You have to teach us
To be gentle with our hearts.

You'll help us summon patience
To conquer earthly hurt.
In time celestial wisdom
Will be softly, surely learnt,
And looking back with hindsight
We shall understand Your words.

Thus, 'Sure of what we hope for
And that we cannot see,'
Our rest will be delivered
Giving us serenity.
Composed amid our trials
We have put our trust in Thee.

## Towards the Light

Off balance at times
In the silent mist
That is my mind,
I search for clarity.

Try to tally reality
And the feelings in my heart.
Fight to align my soul
With our world.

Steadied kindly
By the love around me,
I tread softly
The long road.

Healing takes its time
Of course,
And my journey
Is towards the light.

**Breath of Love**

Feel every heart beat
Breathe every breath
Weep with those weeping
Hold those bereft.

Pray long for answers
Be patient and wait
The Lord's way is perfect
He makes no mistakes.

Love with compassion
All those who are left
Feel every heartbeat
Breathe every breath.

## Hope

Take the long term view.
Now there's a notion!
Easier said than done
Balanced against our short term wishes,
When we are up to our necks in quick sand
And still sinking.

Be responsible.
Now there's another notion!
Get your head round that one
In these days of chronic indifference
And blinkered thoughtlessness
In our quick fix society.

And so we try...

Obligations shape our performance
As we nurse our broken hearts.
Yet hope for a bright future
Moulds our spirits,
As a whisper, from somewhere,
Gives us the grace to be patient.

To wait,
Whilst God weaves,
With iridescent silk,
The ultimate plan
For our very own, eternal,
Happy ending.

# Trying to Make Sense of it All

## Mathew 11 V 28

'Come to me all you who are weary and burdened, and I
will give you rest.'

## Angels

I believe in angels,
I really think that's best.
If you can't believe in angels
Then what about the rest?

Really, truly, deeply,
What is it all about?
And if there is no Jesus
Who calls our time out?

How about the rainbow,
And think about the clouds,
Who could have dreamed up peacocks
And who created flowers?

Who invented music
And the universe and space,
Gave us hearts to dream with
And strength to run the race?

And what if there is no heaven...?

No.
I believe in angels,
I really think that's best.
If you can't believe in angels,
Then what about the rest?

## Turning Point

What's the point?

Starting point
Learning point
Healing point
Turning point

Love's the point

The whole point!

## Acceptance

We fail to understand.
How can we?
Except that we could try
To see the pain of our companions
Through their hurting eyes.
And not inflict our prejudice
Or pre-conceived ideals
Of a world which conforms
To some ghastly norm
Of time and respectability.

There is a limit to our experience.
How do we grasp their grief?
Unless of course we try
Acceptance and belief.
Simple understanding
Of how hard a life can be,
How love was sent to change things
And how that comes down to me.

So if we feed our strangers
And hand out smiles for free,
And spin a web of peace
Around our injured society.
Maybe then, just maybe,
With humility,
We will make the time to listen
And try, at least,
To see.

## Gossip

In our house we have a rule,
If you don't have something good to say
Try not to say it at all.
We exist in a world
Gratuitously cruel
And morals impressed on children
Should register with us all.

What good did gossip ever do?
It just creates unrest.
In each disjointed story
Real chapters face their test.
What pleasure could we ever draw
From writings on the wall
Of real hopes and real wishes
Lost among the dirty dishes?

It's not for us to notice
Mistakes that others make,
We drop enough clangers
Of our own for goodness sake!
Instead let's plan to understand
That underneath the lies
Are people who could use a hand
To heal their fraying lives.

Think of something good to say.
Do something really kind.
Watch the smiles and realise
The joy along that extra mile.
Be the one to recognise
The difference one can make,
When all we really need to do
Is give more than we take.

## Sparkling Prayers

I pray for your angels
To hold hands around
Those whom I love
And those who need love
And those whom I don't even know.

I pray for your light
To shine in the lives
Of those whom I love
Who need to know your love
Who don't even know where to look.

I pray for your truth
To sparkle in me
And capture the souls
Of those who might see
That your space is a good place to be.

I wish for the world
That you wish for too.
The need is so huge Lord,
Reserve me some angels
Please.

## Faith

How does one convey
What cannot be felt
By one's fingers
But only one's heart?

How does one share
The sweet gift of hope
Acceptance
Of what one can't see?

How does one explain
To the rational thinker
The concept of faith
BEFORE knowledge?

## The Tick List

The strangest thing is
That the crashes happen
When you least expect them,
Emotionally that is.

You can be flying along,
Efficiently ticking 'to do's'
From the never ending list
And WALLOP.

You grind to a halt.
All of a sudden
The list doesn't seem to matter
Any more ...

... the ooomph sort of evaporates,
And you wonder for a while
What it's all about
And why?

This, of course, is precisely
When you need God the most.
We all know that, which is fine,
He likes to help.

It's even better however,
If when He has placed you gently
On your feet again,
You acknowledge His love graciously.

Striving to resist
The endless tick list:
Or at the very least,
Letting God write the next one.

## Liberty to Love

God's huge, immovable hand
Draws us a line to stand behind.
It's best this way we usually find
As around us
The world rolls on round.

With patience we begin to see
His huge love gives us liberty.
This is the way He meant it to be
As around us
The world rolls on round.

Accepting this wisdom sets us free
To 'make a difference' genuinely,
Sharing His grace for eternity
As around us
The world rolls on round.

God's huge, immovable hand
Draws us a line to stand behind.
Its best this way we usually find
As around us
The world rolls on round.

## The Gift

And so it is with God
That His present is exquisitely wrapped.
The very way that the pretty lady
In the smartest shop
Deftly wraps as we look on,
Amazed.
And we cannot imagine how she did it?

And so it is with God
That His present is perfectly placed.
Inside the safest cottage,
Underneath the prettiest tree
And next to the warmest fire.
An un-opened Christmas gift,
Wrapped up in a sunset,
Tied with a sky blue ribbon
And sprinkled with the stars.

And so it is with God
That the best is yet to come.
If only we would rest a while
With a smile on our lips
And love in our hearts,
Beginning, ever so slowly and gently,
To reach for our present.

**The Point of the Plot**

OVERLOAD  OVERLOAD
She's breaking up
She's breaking up...

Well actually, she isn't,
But she could
If she doesn't hold tight
To her world
While she still can.

Scrambled?  Me?
Absolutely not.
Oscar winning performances
Day after day
As I pray
For the show to go on.

For the audience to learn
From the beautifully crafted script,
Or was that scriptures?
Or at *least* grasp the point
Of the plot.

Could be a long run
But that's O.K.

So much love along the way
And that's what really counts.

## Comfort

In the confidence of the clouds,
In the beauty of airborne birds,
In the sureness of the sunrise,
I feel your presence.

In the dawning of every day,
In the faithful flow of the tide,
In the comfort of each sunset,
I savour your love.

## A Christian Inheritance

Such a vulnerable place
This space…
And all the while coping with the stark reality
Of the impossible dream.
Contentment and perfect peace
In a world unable to respond
Because the planet, which we inhabit,
Has celestial rules.

We accept our lives graciously,
Nourishing the world afresh
Through the simple happiness of our children.
We capture their joyful smiles,
Treasuring each fleeting moment
As we throw open our windows and doors,
Allowing soothing friendships to blow through,
Bringing their earthly rewards.

We talk with our children while we sit down
And while we walk.
We lead them and nurture them
And keep them safe,
As we try to connect them to matters spiritual.
We give them their share of the celebration
Of birth and death and especially of love,
And the triumph and continuity of it all.

We teach them to cherish our inheritance,
To seek their destiny
And be happy on the way.
We entrust our hopes
And the hearts of all those whom we love,
To His care…
If we dare…
Because we must.

## Contentment

Crises manifest themselves
At arbitrary times
With unusually heavy blows.
Again and again
From somewhere deep inside,
The will to fight emerges from obscurity
With determination.

The Spirit prevails
As strict regimes of self-control
And tiny points of huge purpose
Keep us steady
Against the assault.
Permission to leave refused
We have a job to do.

These times are hard.
No-one exempt.
Most of us know already...and yet
One day, the storm blows away,
The sky forgets to be angry
And the sun eventually remembers to smile.
The acceptance begins...

...Allowing us to fall like children
upon *contentment* as our reward.
The truly discerning among us
Recognising this safe, sweet sense of being,
Transparently wrapped,
And so easily missed,
As the greatest gift of all.

# Treasuring the Good Times

The happy days, the healthy days,
the family days.
The ordinary days, the special days...
the good days!

John 1 v 16

"From the fullness of his grace, we have
all received one blessing after another."

## Friends

Let us be friends my love,
Let us always be friends.
Sharing from time to time
The wonders of this sweet world.

Let us draw from each other
Diamond-studded, gold-star gifts
Of pure energy and infectious joy,
Spreading happiness abroad.

Let us laugh together at life's absurdities.
Non-conformist free spirits,
Softly content in the knowledge
That *we* understand.

Let us bathe in the golden haze
Of perfect companionship.
Let us be friends my love,
Let us always be friends.

## A Happy Soul

Almost without my noticing,
Gently...
Ever so gently
You healed me.
Unzipped my soul
And climbed right in,
Closing it firmly again
Behind you.

Filled now permanently
With warmth and love.
Full, almost to bursting
With all things good
And pure and sweet,
I glow through each day
Like a radioactive beacon,
Intoxicated with happiness.

ALIVE
And most definitely
Still kicking.

## Complete Love

Constant, consistent and complete.
This love is mine
For all time
And I am singing such a happy song...

...of a life full of hope,
Free from doubt, free from fear,
Absolute love, steadfastly near,
Constant, consistent and complete.

## Half a World Away

I know your routine
I can picture the scene
As I sit quietly praying
For you.

Those whom I love
Tucked up in your night
In the midst of my day
Half a world away.

My prayers whispered softly
Ask your safe tomorrow
With summery love
From my warm today.

## Bird Song

I know a little bird,
A very lovely bird
Who has a most important role to play.

She tries to sing sweet songs,
She generally succeeds,
Sometimes people even pause to listen.

I know a little bird,
A quite determined bird
Who will sing until *everyone* has heard.

## Gentle Smiles

I looked in the mirror
But I couldn't see you,
I couldn't even see
The me that you do.

I looked into your eyes
And what did I see?
A soul full of gentle smiles
Reflecting back at me.

## Incorrigible

I can say what I like
As long as it helps
I can do what I like
As long as it heals
I can be what I like
As long as God intends
But I must be happy with me.

I don't have to be mainstream
To make people smile
Or to make people happy
To talk for a while
Or to share their troubles
And bear some away
Or hug them and feed them
And love them today.

I can just be me
The one whom God made
The one he is happy with
(Most of the time)
The one whom he humours
and patiently guides
While easing me gently
through all of my trials.

If I go on listening
He will provide
All that I need to go on being free
To go on being me...
Incorrigible
And staying that way
For all the right reasons.

After all
What can 'they' say
When faced with a smile
So bright that only God could have made it?
There is no such person as 'they'
And I'm glad.

## A Peaceful Future

Such wonder in your quiet presence
A gift of savoured peacefulness
How blessed we are to share this friendship
Sweet and rich in gentleness.

We need not find another future
We need not plan or guess or strive
We need not know our destination
We understand, we have arrived.

## A Safe Place

In this familar, comforting garden
I get off the treadmill to rest,
To be wrapped up in sunshine and daisies
With lavender lining my nest.

A sanctuary, a haven, a safe place
Where peace is a tangible sound,
And comfort and healing and kindness
Are just some of the gifts to be found.

The ceiling is vast and lovely and blue,
The honeysuckle walls smell divine,
The carpet is lush and welcoming green
And the curtains are orange and wine.

The butterflies potter, the dragonflies shine
The wind gently ruffles the trees,
A hammock sways softly, inviting me in
And nobody else ever sees.

If ever there was a time to meet God
A chance to savour his grace,
It is here in this brilliant, magical, beautiful,
Perfectly, wonderful place.

## Occupational Therapy

They say I've had a breakdown,
It hasn't been much fun,
The situation's ludicrous
I'm shocked to have succumbed.

But there we have it, facts are facts
I'm quietly resigned,
The focus is on progress now
Recovery is what's required.

All tasks are to be gentle
Keeping energy preserved,
Nourishment is always crucial
Blood sugars must be observed.

Occupational Therapy
Is really rather good,
I always loved my jigsaws
And did them when I could.

Sewing too is peaceful
And writing soothes the mind,
A glass or two of wine, of course,
Always helps I find.

Then there's rehabilitation,
To the outside world that is,
That can come in many forms
Some of which are bliss.

A visit to an egg farm,
The free range happy kind,
A walk in Wells Cathedral
Where the purest love abides.

A bistro meal in Windsor,
A boat ride on the Thames,
Sir Christopher Wren came up trumps,
His peaceful home a gem.

Coming out of hiding
Is always really tough,
I hope I'm through the worst though
The road's not quite as rough.

My sense of humour works once more
Each smile a healthy sign,
I'd love to have more energy
But that will come in time.

And meanwhile I'll be patient,
Gracious and humble and 'stuff',
At long last I feel confident
That the only way forward is up!

## A New Thing

It took me by surprise, this explosion of love.
When did life start to greet me that way,
With such sweet smiles
And beautiful eyes?

See how the sunlight sparkles
On its dance across the water.
Were flowers as astonishingly vibrant,
Or the heron as elegant in flight, before?
And surely,
Never was the sky so blue?

To begin with,
I did not perceive this new thing
Springing up.
It flowed gracefully,
Pouring peace into my soul
To distract me from my impatience.

With infinite care, God lit His lamp,
And I caught fire.
My heart is now ablaze
And my smile ready.
Real happiness to meet me
At the beginning of each day.

Little wonder then,
At so much love.
How else to respond
To life's riches?

## Unconditional Love

Love a man
Love a woman
Love a child
Love a world
Love yourself
And pass it on.

Search shining eyes,
Unlock hidden compartments.
Revel
In fathomless love
Waiting there,
Smiling.

Stand firm,
Surmount the ordinary,
Bypass convention.
Resolute
In the power
Of unconditional love.

# Things Misplaced

There's a big black hole in our house
Where things just disappear,
Their whereabouts cannot be traced
No sign declaring 'things misplaced'
But we know they are there, somewhere.

I suspect there is one in most homes
Especially those housing kids,
A large list readily springs to mind
Of belongings which we can never find,
But which have to be there, somewhere.

Socks of course are notorious,
Where on earth do they go to hide?
Perhaps the wash basket's in collusion?
Odd socks are certainly no illusion,
But the pairs must be there, somewhere.

Hairbrushes are a fine example
Constant replacements required.
There is simply never one in sight
They seem to vanish over night,
But we know they are there, somewhere.

T.V and video remote controls,
School books (need I say more?),
Reading glasses, biros, selotape and glue,
Do they evaporate in your house too?
Yet they have to be there, somewhere.

No doubt we should try to be tidier,
But I already know that won't work.
That black hole is ravenous,
Greedy and cavernous,
And I *know* it is there, somewhere.

## Everything in Moderation

Everything in moderation
Is probably sound advice,
It's also rather boring,
Like a curry without the spice.

Low fat food is brightly displayed,
At a vastly inflated price,
But I like chips with my fried eggs,
I don't want to eat them with rice.

It's extremely hard to be sensible
When chocolate is just so nice,
And crisps are irresistible,
Multi-packs gone in a trice.

Blackberry and apple crumble?
One helping should suffice,
No giving in to temptation
*Or* the Cornish dairy ice!

A glass of wine is lovely,
A bottle? ( I wouldn't think twice!)
But we mustn't get carried away here
We're not meant to be enticed.

Everything in moderation
Is probably sound advice,
Though what do I think of the sentiment?
'Not much', to be precise.

## Two Thousand and One

*On hearing of the death of the poet Adrian Henri on 20 December 2000*

This year
I want to be well.
I want to do God's will
Willingly.
I want to keep the love I already have
And create some more.
I want to paint 'I love you'
Across the steps of St Andrew's Church
And invite you in.
I want to have at least
25 picnics on the sea front at Felixstowe
In sunshine, at lunchtime.

I want to write letters
And poems which paint pictures.
I want to hug grown-ups
And cuddle children.
I want to bake banana cakes
And spaghetti bolognese.
I want to find sweet posies for gifts
At the W.I. market on Friday mornings.
I want to walk in a bluebell wood.
I want to read more Adrian Henri.
I want to be happy
I
    want
        to
           be
              **ME**

## Rose Tinted Spectacles

I have decided to look at the world
Through the bright eyes of a child.
An especially happy child
Who seizes every chance to smile
And laughs in the rain.
Who talks to the angels
And expects a reply.

I have accepted that this,
Quite simply
Is not a dress rehearsal.
Now I look at the roses
And really see them.
I am enchanted by magic moments as they happen
And I adore them.

I can feel the huge transparent love
All around me.
I am embracing it and sharing it
And calming with it.
I know now that love
Is the best way
To make a difference, today.

So I shall go on looking
Through the eyes of a child,
Wearing my rose-tinted spectacles.
And one day,
When enough of us do the same,
We will fragrance the whole world rose-coloured
And transform it.

## Stranger Things Have Happened

It may sound quite pretentious
But *I've become a poet.*
I have to say I'm rather glad
And I don't mind who knows it.

Stranger things have happened
Than my taking up a pen
And thinking of myself as one
Of literary bent.

Awareness came with gentle words
Which I was thrilled to write,
Amazing inspiration
In the middle of the night.

First one poem, two then three
The verses quickly formed,
And sixty poems later
They are going down a storm.

My dear friend has coached me,
I cribbed notes from his course,
Learned to count in syllables
And bought a large thesaurus.

It seems I have a feel for words
Which stir in people's hearts,
It's vital now to use them
For that's how healing starts.

The right words lead to insight
They ease the way with smiles,
Loving lines alleviate
Life's most testing trials.

So one day I *shall* publish
A requisite poetry book,
Promoting unconditional love
To all who dare to look.

I know God will be pleased with me
For I have listened well.
Who knows? With him behind me,
The book might even sell!